GALAXY OF SUPERSTARS

Ben Affleck
Backstreet Boys
Brandy
Garth Brooks
Mariah Carey
Matt Damon
Cameron Diaz
Leonardo DiCaprio
Céline Dion
Tom Hanks
Hanson
Jennifer Love Hewitt
Lauryn Hill
Jennifer Lopez
Ricky Martin
Ewan McGregor
Mike Myers
'N Sync
LeAnn Rimes
Adam Sandler
Britney Spears
Spice Girls
Jonathan Taylor Thomas
Venus Williams

CHELSEA HOUSE PUBLISHERS

GALAXY OF SUPERSTARS

Adam Sandler

David Seidman

CHELSEA HOUSE PUBLISHERS
Philadelphia

Dedication: *To Mark Conchelos and Mary Seidman. Two people with a great sense of humor who have been patient and gracious when I've dedicated other books to other people. It's about time you got your own book!*

Frontis: *Ignoring harsh critics, Adam Sandler has worked hard to become one of America's top comedians, starring in box-office hits and selling millions of comedy albums.*

Produced by
21st Century Publishing and Communications, Inc.
New York, New York
http://www.21cpc.com

CHELSEA HOUSE PUBLISHERS

Editor in Chief: Stephen Reginald
Managing Editor: James D. Gallagher
Production Manager: Pamela Loos
Art Director: Sara Davis
Director of Photography: Judy L. Hasday
Senior Production Editor: J. Christopher Higgins
Publishing Coordinator/Project Editor: James McAvoy

The Chelsea House World Wide Web address is
http://www.chelseahouse.com

 3 5 7 9 8 6 4 2

Library of Congress Cataloging-in-Publication Data

Seidman, David,
   Adam Sandler / by David Seidman.
      p. cm. — (Galaxy of superstars)
   Includes bibliographical references and index.
   Summary: A biography of the actor-comedian who emerged from "Saturday Night Live" to become a movie superstar in such films as "The Wedding Singer," "Happy Gilmore," and "The Waterboy."
   ISBN 0-7910-5773-9 (hc) — ISBN 0-7910-5774-7 (pb)
   1. Sandler, Adam—Juvenile literature. 2.Actors—United States—Biography—Juvenile literature. [1. Sandler, Adam. 2. Comedians. 3. Actors and actresses.]
I. Title. II. Series.

PN2287.S275 S45 2000
791.43'028'092—dc21
[B]   99-086715
                                                                      CIP
                                                                       AC

CONTENTS

1

ON THE ROAD

A dam Sandler was scared. "Every time I go on stage, I feel panicky," he said years later. "I'm always wondering why I got myself into it. I always swear, 'I don't want to do it, I won't get myself in that situation ever again.'"

In the summer of 1996, Adam was there again: about to face people who expected him to make them laugh.

The show was part of a 12-city comedy concert tour. Adam was playing some of America's biggest, most famous venues, including the Hard Rock Hotel in Las Vegas, the Universal Amphitheater in Los Angeles, and Radio City Music Hall in New York. He was backed by a five-player rock band plus three background singers. The musical group featured high-powered talent: guitarist Waddy Wachtel came from the X-Pensive Winos, the side project of Rolling Stones star Keith Richards, while bassist Bob Glaub had worked with Bob Dylan, Rod Stewart, and Bruce Springsteen. Both musicians had played on *What the Hell Happened to Me?*, Adam's most recent comedy album.

Although his stage presence doesn't betray his fear, Adam Sandler, shown here at the rehersal for the MTV Movie Awards, feels panicky before live audiences. But as is true for most stand-up comedians, life on the road is essential to keeping his career alive.

Adam refuses to pull his punches simply to satisfy critics who charge that he is tasteless, humorless, and offensive.

The tours and records were only a small part of Adam's world. He had just starred in the action-comedy movie *Bulletproof*, made a guest appearance on *Saturday Night Live*, gone to the record industry's Grammy Awards (where another of his records, the million-selling *they're all gonna laugh at you*, was nominated for Best Comedy Album) and begun dating teenage actress Alicia Silverstone (*Clueless*). And his recent movie *Happy Gilmore* was one of the country's biggest hits.

With all of his successes, not to mention his 12 years of performing comedy professionally, then-29-year-old Adam shouldn't have been nervous —but he was. Still, he had a show to do.

Adam sprinted out onto the stage to the enthusiastic cheers of several thousand teenagers and college students. He started at full energy, rumbling and shrieking out songs from his albums. He sang "My Little Chicken," a song expressing bizarre desire for a barnyard animal, and "Lunchlady Land," a silly trip back to his school days in Manchester, New Hampshire. The crowd loved it all.

He used almost every inch of the stage, which looked like a high-school kid's yard: basketball hoop, chain-link fence, and the back porch of a suburban house. He went to the porch to talk to his mother (played by Adam himself), only to find her doing various outrageous and sometimes obscene things.

Much of the show was pretty tasteless but not all of it. At one point pictures of various Jewish celebrities flashed on a large screen on the stage while Adam sang his popular "Chanukah Song."

The show took one strange twist after another, with Adam behaving like a goofy whirlwind. The critics were especially savage in their reviews; they attacked almost everything that he did. They may have underestimated him, though. Adam was not really just the overgrown teenager that he played onstage, in film, and in front of the television cameras. He was more. A lot more.

2

FUNNY FROM THE START

"**H**e's always been funny; he always woke up in a good mood. We knew he would be an entertainer." Those are the words of Judy Sandler, and she should know. Adam is her son.

Judy was a nice, single Jewish girl when one of her friends fixed her up on a blind date with a nice Jewish boy—a guy named Stan Sandler. "After that, there was nobody else but him," she said years later. The two got married and settled down in Brooklyn, New York. Stan, an electrical engineer, brought home the paycheck; Judy was the homemaker. Kids soon followed: Elizabeth, Valerie, Scott, and finally, on September 9, 1966, Adam.

Judy was the first to encourage Adam's talent—but not as a comedian. Around age 3, Adam would sing in a voice somewhat like that of a character that he'd make famous on *Saturday Night Live*, Operaman. She even sent Adam to singing lessons. "And that didn't work out too well because I always would rather be playing baseball than singing in a room with an old lady," Adam said.

It didn't take Adam long to move from singing to comedy.

From the start, Adam always made people laugh, and events from his childhood often show up in his work. He is shown at the Big Daddy *premiere with twin costars, Cole and Dylan Sprouse, who played his son.*

"One of my first impressions was my dad's sneeze. It used to make my mom laugh," Adam recalled. Judy agreed: "He always made people laugh. I could scold Adam, and by the time I was all finished, we were laughing."

Stan Sandler may not have taken Adam's comedy so well. In interviews, Adam has always praised Stan: "He was always the coolest dad. He did everything for his kids, and he never made us feel like he was pressured." However, his comedy tells another story.

Adam's stand-up act has included an impression of Stan at the dinner table, yelling "Shut up!" During his years in one of the messiest offices at *Saturday Night Live*, Adam said, "If my dad saw this office, there would be a red face and a long stare. 'What's the matter with you? Get a hold of your life!'" When Adam was asked in 1999 what he'd do if he were president, he answered, "Yell at my father. Tell him he can't yell back because I'm the president. And then laugh at him." And the films that Adam has written often feature father figures whom he has to work hard to please.

Stan could be sensitive, though. Adam remembered, "When I lost my Diver Dan doll, my dad dressed up as Diver Dan's dad and came to the front door. He said the doll was with him now, but thanks for watching it while he grew up. Dad would do anything to make me feel better." Adam put the memory in his movie *Big Daddy*.

Not long after the Diver Dan incident, Stan and Judy made a change that influenced the rest of Adam's life. When Adam was six, the family moved to Manchester, New Hampshire.

Manchester is a manufacturing center big in electrical equipment, making it a great place

for an engineer like Stan. It's the state's largest city, although with 100,000 people, it's no megalopolis. The nearest truly big town is Boston, more than 50 miles south.

In a quiet, prosperous-looking residential area of Manchester, near the top of a gently sloping rise, sits the Sandler home on Madeline Road. It's a wide, brown house behind a green lawn, thick ferns, and needle-leafed trees.

Adam had a normal life. "He dressed in fatigues for tomato wars with his friends, posted [model] Cheryl Tiegs on his bedroom wall," journalist Kate Meyers reported in *Entertainment Weekly*, "[and] played Little League shortstop." He entered Punt, Pass, and Kick football

A quiet New Hampshire gas station and general store on an autumn day. Growing up in Manchester, a small town in New Hampshire, Adam was known for screaming jokes during movies and making the whole audience laugh.

tournaments and won at age eight because "I was the only kid in my age bracket." He wanted so much for his mother to be proud of his victory that for more than 20 years he didn't tell her how he won.

Take a short walk down Madeline Road and turn the corner, and there you'll see Webster Elementary School, where Adam spent six years.

He was no teacher's pet. In the first grade, Adam would ask his teacher to be excused, and he'd run home. Instead of demanding to know why Adam wasn't in school, Judy would make him a sandwich and walk him back to class. He became a gutsy kid who'd take any dare. He wasn't a bad boy, though. "I [just] talked too much, yelled too much, and I got in trouble for just being loud."

While he could be funny in school, "the funniest stuff I did when I was little, first to sixth grade, was at movie theaters, screaming at the screen and making the whole theater laugh. I'd always say like five jokes, and there would be four power laughs. The fifth one, I would say, 'Hey, nice hair!' or something like that, and somebody would go, 'Hey, shut up!'"

Adam's brother Scott has said that Adam was "perpetually performing." At age seven, Adam, in an impromptu performance, sang the song "The Candy Man" for the patients at a Manchester nursing home. Judy encouraged him. "She would ask him to sing 'Maria' from *West Side Story* [to her], and he would," Scott recalled. Adam was still singing it for his mother more than 20 years later.

"The first time I was on stage was at my sister's wedding," Adam has said. "I was 11 or 12, and I sang 'You're Sixteen,' Ringo Starr's version of that. I knew all the lyrics to it, and that went over all right. Then I sang 'Yesterday,' by Paul McCartney. Things started to go downhill. 'One was enough,' they said."

Around that time, Adam also did his first onstage performance for people who weren't relatives. He sang the bluesy "House of the Rising Sun" in a seventh-grade talent show. "I remember my mother driving me home afterward, and she said, 'You kept cracking your voice.' So she thought I didn't sell it. But I thought I did a pretty good job."

Though performing was fun, life offstage was tough. Adam graduated from Webster and went to Hillside Junior High School. No longer could he walk to school; Hillside was further away, which meant sprinting out of the house to catch a school bus, and he was usually running late. Adam also faced anti-Semitic comments from the other kids. "It would hurt," Adam has said. "Every day on the bus, I was ready to hear some stupid comment made."

Stan helped Adam handle the situation. "My dad would talk about [movie star] Kirk Douglas and tell me he's Jewish. I'd say, 'That's good.' I didn't feel so alone." Later, Adam would write "The Chanukah Song," partly to let kids in his position know that they too aren't alone.

Stan also had more forceful advice for his son. "My dad always told me if a kid made a Jewish comment, I should give him a little hitting and remind him, 'If you're going to say something stupid, you'll pay for it,'" Adam has remembered.

Like other boys, Adam also discovered girls. "My sixth-grade girlfriend was one of my first kisses. . . ." He also learned about heartbreak. "One time a girl broke up with me in sixth grade on the phone when I was eating dinner with my family. . . . I stared at my plate and tried not to cry the whole dinner."

With all these distractions, Adam's schoolwork slipped. "In the first through sixth grade, I got some nice grades, but then I turned into a wise guy," he said years later. "Instead of being book smart, I decided to have fun."

His parents disliked the change. "One time, my mother was yelling, 'Why don't you ever try?'" Adam recalled. "I had a tape recorder in my hand. When she stopped shouting, I played it back at her. She laughed for half an hour."

However, his father was harder to handle. "I couldn't make eye contact with my dad at report-card time."

The only indication of Adam's future was an interest in humor. He loved the sometimes profane comedy of the movies *Blazing Saddles* and *Young Frankenstein*, the frat-boy laughs of *Animal House*, and the gag-a-minute silliness of *Airplane!* He liked Jerry Lewis, who often played a childish adult, and Abbott and Costello, a team in which one of the partners played, yes, a childish adult—a type that Adam would play on-screen in later years.

But his favorite was the comedian who moans, "I can't get no respect"—the pop-eyed sad sack, Rodney Dangerfield. Adam has talked about seeing Dangerfield's 1980 golf comedy *Caddyshack* 30 times. "I'd walk around my house doing Rodney jokes for my dad."

The jokes didn't always work. "Looking back, I wasn't really that funny. I was like this little annoying kid. My parents would laugh at my jokes and then walk away shaking their heads."

After leaving Hillside, Adam went to Central High School. At Central, Adam continued playing the annoying goof. "Adam was just like Bart

Simpson," says Michael Clemons, Adam's U.S. Government teacher. Principal Bob Schiavone added, "Teachers would ask him to leave the class, but they were laughing while they asked. He was hilarious."

And popular. "The students always invited him to whatever they were doing because they wanted to see what he was going to do," Schiavone said. Adam was named Class Clown in his senior year, played junior-varsity basketball, and served on the student council.

He also played in a band, variously named Spectrum, Storm, and Final Warning. Judy remembered letting the band practice in the basement, even though "the dishes used to rattle, and the dog had a nervous breakdown with all the noise." Adam added, "I just remember jamming downstairs very loud on, like, a Black Sabbath song, and my mom would come downstairs and clap along."

Like many students, Adam took part-time jobs. Unfortunately, he said, "Growing up, I wasn't that great at anything." The jobs didn't last.

Eventually Scott became a lawyer, Elizabeth a dentist, and Valerie a food-company executive. Adam, on the other hand, seemed to have no direction. But all that changed in 1984.

3

STANDING UP
FOR HIMSELF

"I was 17, applying for colleges and stuff. I said, 'What am I gonna do [with my life]?'" Adam has remembered. Scott, then a Boston University student, pushed him to go to an open-mike night at the Boston comedy club Stitches. "If he hadn't said to do it, I wouldn't have thought it was a normal thing to do," Adam recalled.

For new comedians, open-mike nights are pure hell. Comedians sign up to do five-minute sets at no pay. Most of the people in the audience are drunk or, worse, other comedians. They rarely laugh at their competitors' work.

Adam had a typically rough time. "I remember going onstage, not knowing what to do, hearing some 'drunk guy slurring, 'He's got a retainer!'"

Most comedians develop insults to quiet the loud-mouths, but not Adam. "I could never think of anything. It would be more like [whining], 'Please, I'm trying to speak.'"

Nevertheless, Adam was hooked. "It was the first time in my life where I said, 'All right. I think I can [do this].'" Besides, for Adam, comedy seemed easier than a real job. "There was nothing else I could do, nothing else I could

---

While attending New York University, adjoining Washington Square Park, shown here, Adam performed stand-up comedy at New York City area nightclubs. His routines were awful, but he was hooked because he finally found something he could put his heart into.

put my heart into."

Comedy is an uncertain profession, but Stan and Judy didn't mind much. "I think they were relieved I had something to get into, because we were all wondering what the hell I was going to do with my life."

To pursue comedy, Adam went to New York University. The school was close to some of New York's comedy clubs. Even better, the entrance requirements for NYU's acting program were lower than those for its other departments.

In his freshman year, Adam roomed with pre-law student Tim Herlihy, who shared Adam's taste in comedy. "The reason we were first friends is that I couldn't believe some of the stuff coming out of his mouth," Herlihy said. "It's the stuff we think but don't say."

Herlihy and other NYU students became Adam's friends. "They amused themselves blasting Led Zeppelin tunes and pulling childish pranks—like putting an amplifier in their window and shouting, 'Hey, you! Baldy!' to pedestrians below," *People* magazine's Karen Schneider has reported.

Adam did stand-up at places like the Dive, an NYU nightclub. The club let him go onstage not because he was a great comic but because he brought an audience—his friends —at $2 a head.

Even with buddies nearby, stand-up terrified Adam, and he was full of anxiety before and after each performance. "It would ruin my whole week if I knew on Monday that I had a show on Friday. . . . It would take me two weeks to recover." He had no confidence in himself—"I was trying too hard in the beginning to be like other comedians but eventually discovered my own style of comedy."

His fear showed on the stage. "I would be very nervous. I couldn't concentrate; my thoughts were scattered. I froze in front of audiences." Even when he could speak, "I'd get a shaky voice, like I was about to cry." Sometimes, he was too scared even to look at the audience. "I'd stand there, show after show, and wonder why I'd gotten into this industry. I hated when people looked at me, and I would actually feel sick from nervousness."

But he didn't quit. "My friends were always around to say, 'Hey, Sandler, you're funnier than that,' and that's what kept me going. They were always there to tell me that I was a funny guy."

Brother Scott offered support, too. Adam recalled, "Sometimes, I'd get so panicked that I would stutter. My brother said, 'You should sing more. Then, you'd know exactly what words to use, and you could relax more.'" That advice would pay off brilliantly in the future.

In addition to doing stand-up, Adam acted in student films directed by a friend, NYU student Frank Coraci. He worked in a drugstore but got fired for miscounting pills. He also worked as a waiter and a dishwasher: "I'm working with Brazilian guys who speak only Portuguese. I kept trying to make them laugh." He even sang in subways.

He didn't have to sing for long. According to published reports, Adam met Lorenzo Quinn, son of Oscar-winning actor Anthony Quinn. The elder Quinn in turn introduced Adam to Bill Cosby of TV's *The Cosby Show*. Thanks to *Cosby Show* casting director Barry Moss, who later became Adam's agent, Adam was hired for a few episodes to play Smitty, a not-too-bright friend of Cosby's TV son, Theo.

In addition to being a sitcom king, Bill Cosby

Adam played the role of Smitty on a few episodes of The Cosby Show, *but when Bill Cosby, one of the great comedians of his generation, heard Adam do stand-up, he was reportedly turned off by the obscene material.*

was one of the greats of stand-up. He wanted to see Adam's act. The act was obscene, and Adam wasn't sure if the old-fashioned Cosby would like it. According to published reports, "Cosby didn't laugh. He merely stared and said, 'You can't do that. You're not going to get anywhere with that stuff.'"

In addition to performing on *The Cosby Show* and in various comedy clubs, Adam took acting classes at the Lee Strasberg Theater Institute, whose alumni include some of the world's top actors.

"He was terrible," Strasberg instructor Mel Gordon has said. "Focus and concentration— that's what Adam was lacking the most. He was always looking out the window."

Adam recalled, "Everyone else was pretty intense, whipping out the names of play- wrights. We're all supposed to go onstage and dig out our emotions. At that time, I couldn't even look another person in the eye. I'm think- ing, 'Once I dig out my emotions, where do they go?'" Adam was such a misfit that Gordon gave him some fatherly advice: quit show business.

Adam didn't quit. He kept working, doing stand-up as many as six nights a week. "I'd see him work on [a piece of his act] for a few weeks and finally figure out how to make it work," Coraci recalled. Adam himself admitted, "It took at least four years working in the comedy clubs until I believed [I was funny]."

"His jokes would bomb all the time, but he would never bomb," said Lucien Hold, talent manager for the comedy club Comic Strip. "It was more about his own personality up there. He was so likable."

Adam eventually graduated from NYU with a degree in fine arts. But, in 1988, before he graduated, he got a great job. The cable net- work MTV began producing *Remote Control.*

Remote Control was a parody of TV game shows. Adam played recurring characters who told stories that turned into questions for the contestants. As the shirtless, European-accented Stud Boy, he asked the contestants to identify famous women based on his encounters with them. He also played the bully Stickpin.

Soon after its premiere in early 1988, *Remote Control* became MTV's top-rated series, eventu- ally airing more than 300 episodes. "That was a great time," Adam said years later. "We went on the road for *Remote Control*, and we did all these colleges. I just felt a little bit like what a rock 'n' roll guy would feel."

Things got even better when, at a comedy club in New York, he met Margaret Ruden, a cosmetics-company marketing executive. The two fell in love. Unfortunately, they couldn't always be together. After *Remote Control* ended, Adam headed to the movie and TV mecca: Los Angeles.

"His act was not what we'd call A-1 material," said Budd Friedman, founder of Los Angeles comedy club The Improv. "It was more about his attitude, his little-boy quality, his vulnerability." "He had this really innocent look," said Jamie Masada, who owned the Laugh Factory club. "Everyone wanted to be his friend."

Some of them did become his friends, like young comics Rob Schneider and Jon Stewart. Adam remembered, "It was like we were all best friends. We did everything together." They later worked with Adam in unexpected ways.

Adam's stand-up work led to his first movie. In the low-budget *Babes Ahoy* (also known as *Going Overboard*), Adam played a cruise-ship waiter who wants to be a comedian. According to *Los Angeles Times* reporter Daniel Cerone, the movie took "three days to write, a day to cast, two days to prepare and a week of on-board shooting plus two days of pick-up shots" —an amazingly short time, given that most movies take months or years to make. The movie didn't make it into wide release.

If Adam cared much, he hasn't publicly said so. When the movie finished, he returned to stand-up. "All I did was concentrate on my stand-up comedy and making sure I was good

When Adam met Margaret Ruden at a New York City comedy club, he immediately fell in love. The couple, shown here in 1992, kept up their relationship for a long time even though they lived on opposite coasts after Adam moved to Los Angeles. The distance, however, proved to be too much, and they eventually broke up.

at that and making sure I would get on stage no matter where I was. I would never say no to a show because I'd feel too guilty that it could have been a thing that helped me get better at my job."

The job didn't include neatness. "I have all my stand-up jokes written on six pieces of paper," he said. "They're just beat-up, really old and all smudged, with the tiniest writing."

Those six pieces of paper led to Adam's biggest opportunity yet.

4

LIVE FROM NEW YORK . . .

S ince age 17, Adam had dreamed of being on NBC's *Saturday Night Live (SNL)*. From the late-night comedy show's birth in 1975, young comedians came into it unknown and emerged famous: Eddie Murphy, Mike Myers of the *Austin Powers* movies, Jane Curtin of the TV series *Third Rock from the Sun*, and many others.

Dennis Miller hosted *SNL*'s "Weekend Update," a fake newscast that made fun of the week's events. Lorne Michaels, *SNL*'s creator and executive producer, listened when Miller recommended a young stand-up comedian he'd seen in Los Angeles: Adam Sandler.

Michaels went to see Adam's stand-up routine, and he liked it. He auditioned then-23-year-old Adam for *SNL* and hired him for the 1990–91 season—not as a performer but as a writer. "I wasn't sure what that meant," Adam later confessed. It meant his new job was to invent sketches (short playlets), phony TV commercials, monologues, and other comedy bits. Adam joined a staff of about 15 other writers and found himself under great pressure.

"His comedy was probably jarring to some people at

Adam got a big break as part of New York City's entertainment scene when Lorne Michaels hired him as a writer for Saturday Night Live. *In just one year, Adam rose from writer, to featured performer, to cast member.*

As a cast member at SNL, Adam (back row, left) formed lasting friendships with Chris Farley (front row, left), Rob Schneider (middle row, right), and David Spade (back row, next to Adam). He relied on them for honest criticism.

first because the cast was uniformly of a certain generation, then in comes this guy in his mid-20s," said Conan O'Brien, who at the time was also a writer for the show. As Michaels put it, "I'm 48, and I'm talking to writers who are 23. They're suggesting an idea, and I'm thinking, 'We've done that five or six times, and it hasn't worked *ever*!'"

The show had to be written, rehearsed, and performed live on the air week after week. Adam spent up to 18 hours a day working. "Doing *Saturday Night Live* definitely affects my relationship with my girlfriend and with my family, because you feel so much pressure to do well," he admitted.

Fortunately, Adam started making friends among the younger staff. *SNL* writer-actor Rob Schneider was already a pal from Adam's days in stand-up. Another young stand-up, writer-actor David Spade, shared an office with Adam, and the two became close. Yet another new buddy was *SNL* rookie Chris Farley, a wild man who came from Second City, a comedy company based in Chicago, Illinois. The fun-loving Farley nicknamed his pal "Adsy" and appealed to the part of Adam that loved prank phone calls and other misbehavior.

Many of the characters that Adam thought up were so weird that the cast members weren't eager to portray them. He refused to change them. "Adam was very confident about the kinds of things that he thought were funny, and he wasn't about to water it down for anybody," says O'Brien. So, finally, Adam performed them himself.

Live TV terrified him. "Sitting with [host] Tom Hanks ten seconds before the lights come up on my first skit on the air, I said, 'I might faint. There is a good chance I'm going to faint.' Hanks looks over, real concerned, and says, 'Well, don't.'"

Moreover, Adam didn't fully understand acting. "I don't know what happens," he said. "When I get into costume, my personality changes."

Nonetheless, Adam became a stand out. His first hit was Operaman, who spoke only in singsongy mock-Italian that rhymed.

Operaman, Adam later explained, came from

"[a] guy from 57th Street, some guy [who] sings opera and gets money in a cup. I just used to do an impression of him." Writers Bonnie and Terry Turner took Adam's creation and made him a commentator on "Weekend Update." The audience loved him.

Another "Weekend Update" character of Adam's was Cajunman. Cajunman spoke only a few words, and they all ended with *-on*. He was inspired by an actual Cajun, Adam remembered: "My friends and I had gone to a restaurant, and there was this Cajun guy in front of us who had a 'reserva-*tion*.'" Cajunman chatted with new "Weekend Update" anchor Kevin Nealon, whom he called "Kev-*on*."

With characters like these, Adam took a step forward by moving from writer to featured performer, and then he was invited to become a cast member—all in one year.

Most of his early work was presentational; that is, he talked to the audience, just as he did in his stand-up act. He didn't have much experience in sketch comedy, so he didn't do it much at first. But the more he tried it, the more he began to succeed at it.

In one recurring sketch, Adam, Farley, and Spade played the Gap Girls, a gaggle of clothing salesgirls who offered customers any article of clothing, no matter how poorly it fit or how bad it looked on them. For example, if a customer was reluctant to buy a pair of pants that were obviously far too big on them, Adam's character would blithely advise, "Just get a belt, and you cinch 'em!" The Girls spent more time being snippy with each other than selling, though. When Farley sniped at Spade, Adam begged them to be nice in a breathless falsetto that sounded close to tears. The audience adored him.

Sketches also let Adam deliver his most con-
troversial *SNL* character, the fumbling Canteen
Boy, who is based on at least one acquaintance
from Adam's boyhood. "He's not retarded; he's
just a silly kid who stayed in the Scouts too
long," Adam explained about the character.
Canteen Boy was a naive, overgrown Boy
Scout. Adam continued, "The reason you feel
bad for him and you can laugh is because he,
and I guess a lot of my characters, they don't
notice they're getting made fun of." One
Canteen Boy sketch brought in 58 phone calls
from offended viewers. (By comparison, the

*One of Adam's most
successful SNL sketches
featured him with
David Spade (left) and
Chris Farley (right) as
the Gap Girls, sales
clerks who encouraged
customers to buy cloth-
ing no matter how bad
it looked on them.*

rest of that night's show brought in only eight complaints.)

Canteen Boy wasn't the only thing about Adam that annoyed some viewers. One watched him and wrote, "What are you, age eight? . . . Die soon." The *New Yorker's* James Wolcott wrote, "Adam Sandler (he does the annoying Opera Man), with his baseball cap worn backward and his acorn head, is a Gap ad gone wrong." Another showbiz journalist disdainfully called Adam "a symbol of everything that has gone haywire in the world of comedy."

Adam kept on working. He continued to find rich comedy in holidays. During a "Weekend Update" near Halloween, he showed trick-or-treaters how to create quick, low-cost costumes. He stuck his hand in a shoe and growled, "Hi, I'm Crazy Sneaker Hand. Now, gimme some *candy!*" He hung a teabag over his face: "I'm Crazy Teabag-Face Man! Gimme some *candy!*" On he went, putting a pickle in his sleeve and using other silly props.

Adam combined his talent for holiday-based comedy with his love of music to create some of his most popular presentations. There was the silly "Thanksgiving Song," the irreverent "Chanukah Song," and the sinister "Christmas Song" with lyrics like "Santa won't be coming to my house this year, 'Cause I tried to drown my sister and I pierced my ear."

Slowly but surely, Adam began gaining admirers. *Newsweek* called him inspired, and *Entertainment Weekly* absolutely loved him, saying, "He's likely to be SNL's next breakout star." At the end of his first season, Adam and *SNL*'s other writers were nominated for an Emmy Award. His performance of "Red-Hooded Sweatshirt," a song that he wrote to celebrate a beloved piece of childhood clothing, made it onto the home video *Saturday Night Live: The Best of 1992.*

But it didn't take long for Adam to realize that *SNL* alone couldn't satisfy him.

5

GOOD-BYE SNL,
HELLO RECORDS AND MOVIES

66 **I** 'm not a dumb guy with my career," Adam said during his *SNL* days. "People like you the most when they're discovering you, because you're *their* discovery. . . . But then I know it's going to go away, that connection."

Adam was determined to build on his fans' affection before it could fade. "He was always ambitious, and he was very impatient," said Barry Moss. (Adam eventually left Moss and signed with Bernie Brillstein, who also represented Lorne Michaels and other *SNL* powerhouses.) "He'd want to start a movie tomorrow."

Adam virtually did just that. In 1991, he played a small role in *Shakes the Clown*, a movie about a dysfunctional funnyman. He appeared briefly in *Coneheads*, a 1993 movie based on *SNL* sketches about space aliens in suburbia. And he tried out for the 1992 flop *Brain Donors*, auditioning five times, but the part went to actor John Turturro. The process did, however, acquaint him with the movie's director, Dennis Dugan, who later directed Adam's movies *Happy Gilmore* and *Big Daddy*.

Using the fame he gained from SNL, *Adam accepted several movie roles that were generally hated by critics. After the box-office success of* Billy Madison, *which Adam both wrote and starred in, he left* SNL *and moved to Hollywood to focus on his movie career.*

He continued doing stand-up, particularly during *SNL*'s summer breaks. He appeared at the Just For Laughs comedy festival in Montreal, was filmed for the Fox stand-up TV series *Comic Strip* in San Francisco, opened for *SNL* star Dana Carvey's stand-up show in San Diego, and headlined with David Spade in Atlanta and Chicago, among other places. In Toronto, he faced a comedian's nightmare, though: he was told to do a 40-minute set when he had prepared only 20 minutes of material. He bombed.

The project that seemed to excite him most was his first album. "I had the kind of total control over this material that I would never have on TV or in a movie. There's a side of me that's just impossible for NBC to air, and that's what ended up on the record."

Recorded in the summer of 1993 in both New York and Southern California, *they're all gonna laugh at you!* included Adam's popular "Thanksgiving Song" and such new cuts as "The Beating of a High School Janitor" and "My Little Chicken."

The album was an *SNL* family affair. Rob Schneider, Conan O'Brien, and David Spade performed on it, along with *SNL* writer-performers Tim Meadows and Robert Smigel. Adam's pal Tim Herlihy and girlfriend Margaret Ruden participated as well.

"The result is a heartbreaking disappointment. It's simply not very funny," said critic David Mills in the *Washington Post*.

Even Adam's family disliked the record. It was so obscene that "me and my mother, after her hearing the album, avoid eye contact," Adam said. "My older brother likes the album, but my two sisters and my parents don't even acknowledge it."

The public seemed to enjoy the album, though. It sold over a million copies.

Even though Adam's career was taking off, he began running into a problem. He found himself lonely in places where he used to feel at home. He tried not to let these feelings show. With friends like Chris Farley, though, he was another person. "When we're alone, we can be sensitive. But when other people are around, we start talking about [obscene] stuff to let 'em know we're still funny."

Funny he was. In 1994, he played a dopey but lovable rock drummer in the film *Airheads*. He based his performance on the drummer in his high-school band. The movie's lead actor was Brendan Fraser, later to star in *George of the Jungle* and *The Mummy*. To Fraser, Adam

Adam's role in Airheads *earned him mixed reviews.* Rolling Stone *proclaimed him a "red-hot screen find," but* Entertainment Weekly *called him obnoxious.*

was like an amusement-park ride: "You experience Adam. There's one and there's ten, and [with Adam] you get ten all the time. There's no two and nine." Costar Amy Locane agreed, and *People* magazine reported, "She grows flushed when speaking of Adam Sandler. . . . 'He's very cool,' she gushes."

"What a goof" was Adam's response to the idea of being a sex symbol. "I wake up in the morning, look in the mirror and I just go, 'Why? Why do you look like that?'"

The critics' reviews of Adam's performance in *Airheads* were mixed. *Entertainment Weekly* called Adam obnoxious, while Peter Travers of *Rolling Stone* dubbed him "a red-hot screen find."

After *Airheads* came *Mixed Nuts*, a movie in which Adam got a bigger job than he'd signed on for. Writer-director Nora Ephron liked him and let him create extra lines and songs. The critics didn't like Adam as much as Ephron did. The show-biz bible *Variety* called him "just plain irritating."

Neither *Airheads* nor *Mixed Nuts* made much money in theaters. Nevertheless, Universal Studios decided to take a chance on Adam, who speculated that Jim Carrey was partly responsible. Like Adam, Carrey was best known as a player on a sketch-comedy TV show (*In Living Color*). Then he made the slapstick movie *Ace Ventura, Pet Detective*. It was a hit, earning almost $35 million at the box office. Carrey's success, Adam speculated, "lets Hollywood take a chance on newer guys."

Teaming up with his friend Tim Herlihy, Adam wrote *Billy Madison*, a zany movie about a goof-off who bribed his way through school. The adult Billy must prove himself to his father by passing grades one through 12 in only a few months. Along the way, Billy pummels his first-grade classmates in a vicious game of dodge ball and celebrates Nudie Magazine Day.

It was Adam's most familiar kind of comedy. "When I write, I write about growin' up. And I always thought that going through first to twelfth grade again would be a good way to use a lot of that [material] at once."

Adam peppered the film with friends like Chris Farley and Robert Smigel. An old NYU buddy, Jack Giarraputo, was the associate producer. For the most important job, the movie's director, Adam got Universal to hire another friend: Stephen Kessler, who up to that point had primarily directed TV commercials.

Universal fired Kessler early on. "The studio wanted a less stylized movie, more of me being a goof," Sandler said. "It was very sad, like breaking up with a girlfriend." Kessler was replaced by Tamra Davis, director of the rap parody *CB4*.

Davis found that her star cared passionately about the movie. "He'd call me every night after dailies (film from each day's shooting), and we'd talk about the movie for an hour," she said. Adam confessed, "Billy's the closest I've come to playing myself. I feel so much pressure because I want it to be as good as it can be." He took part in editing the movie—an area where actors and writers are usually not involved—and enjoyed the process: "It reminded me of when I did my [first] album."

In February 1995, Universal released the film. *Time* movie critic Richard Schickel called it "one of the most execrable movies ever made." *Variety*'s Brian Lowry wrote, "[Sandler]

While fans loved Adam's role in Billy Madison, *some of the critics predicted the movie would end his film career. Instead, the film made Adam a star.*

mugs, struts and sings but never really comes close to acting." *Rolling Stone's* Peter Travers predicted that *Billy* would "speed [Adam's] film career to a premature end."

The star himself wasn't sure about *Billy*'s fate. He's admitted driving to theaters when the movie opened to find out if people were going to see it.

Indeed they were. In its first weekend, *Billy* was America's top box-office hit, earning about $7 million. It eventually earned more than $25 million and made Adam a star.

Meanwhile, his album *they're all gonna laugh at you!* was still selling very well. The National Academy of Recording Arts and Sciences nominated it for a Best Comedy Album Grammy Award.

Adam's personal life was going strong, too. Early in 1995, he proposed marriage to Margaret Ruden. "I just popped it out," he said. "I wanted to make sure she knew I loved her."

With success in almost every area, Adam was growing disenchanted with *Saturday Night Live*. Strong writers like Bonnie Turner, Terry Turner, and Róbert Smigel had left the show. He was pleased, however, that, based on his recommendation, *SNL* hired his long-time friend Tim Herlihy as one of the new writers.

Some *SNL* staffers got mad at Adam when he allegedly used the studio to record a birthday song for movie kingpin Steven Spielberg. New *SNL* writer-performer Janeane Garofalo ridiculed Adam's characters as "childish," infuriating him. Finally, Adam felt that he was starting to repeat himself on the show and was getting bored.

Shortly after July 4, 1995, Adam quit *SNL*. It was not an easy time. "I kept thinking, 'My life is going to be different. I wonder if it will be okay.'" Fortunately, he wasn't alone. "Me and Farley left together, which made it easier. We'd talk on the phone all the time and say, 'Are we going to be all right? Is this going to be okay?'"

He had nothing to worry about.

6

THE BIG TIME

Adam stayed out of the public eye, working with Tim Herlihy on writing his next movie, *Happy Gilmore*. They also got help from another friend and ex-roommate, writer Judd Apatow, who had worked on comedies such as Jim Carrey's hit *Liar Liar*. *Happy* featured Adam as a hard-charging hockey player named Happy who could hit a golf ball an amazing 400 yards.

Happy was in some part inspired by *Caddyshack*, in which Rodney Dangerfield played a loudmouthed lout who infuriated the snobs who dominated the links, and in part by Stan Sandler's love of golf. The lead character came from a hockey-playing childhood pal of Adam's, Kyle McDonough. "One time, my dad brought Kyle and me to the driving range," Adam remembered. "[Kyle] whacked the ball 100 yards farther than anyone. I wanted to put that hockey mentality on the golf course."

Part of the hockey mentality was violence. "If a guy misses a putt [in conventional golf], the most he usually does is curse and throw a club. Happy punches his opponents in the face," Adam explained.

Adam's movie Happy Gilmore, *in which he starred with Bob Barker (left), placed in the top 20 percent of movies released in 1996 and set the stage for Adam to reach the big time.*

Creating a hot-tempered lead character was a risk, and Adam knew it. "Tim and I were looking for that edge to the character, but we did a lot of thinking before we actually decided to give him a bad temper. We were aware that we were in danger of creating a character that people won't like."

Happy wasn't the only chance that Adam took. In the film, he fights with 72-year-old game-show host Bob Barker. "I was a little tentative with Bob in the beginning until I noticed he was roughhousing me," Adam said. "I heard my neck crack, and I said to myself, 'This guy means business.'"

Being a golfer himself—he shot in the high 90s, quite a respectable record—Adam used the film's golf-course locations to have fun. "Me and [costars] Carl Weathers and Chris McDonald would always ask the [crew] guys, 'How long is it going to take to set up?' and then run away to the green and chip," Adam said. "It's the most fun I ever had on a movie set."

Adam hoped that *Happy* would expand his audience. "*Happy*," he explained, "is one of the first things [I've done] that, if you're 40, you might not be bummed out sitting through it." After all, the hero loved his grandmother and got beaten by the elderly Barker.

The critics were, as usual, vicious. While the *Hollywood Reporter*'s Michael Rechtshaffen called the movie "amicable entertainment," *Variety*'s Brian Lowry said that the entire movie had "about three minutes of funny material" adding, "Sandler remains a thoroughly grating onscreen personality with zero acting range."

Happy was released to theaters in February 1996. It earned more than $38 million at the box office and ended 1996 as one of the 40 most popular movies of the nearly 280 films released that year.

While Adam was working on *Happy*, he was also preparing his next album, *What the Hell Happened to Me?* On this project, he worked with *SNL* colleagues Kevin Nealon, who also appeared in *Billy Madison*, plus old pals Tim Herlihy, Judd Apatow, and Frank Coraci.

Adam began work on the record with his usual dedication. "I honestly was in a room three to four months, six or seven days a week, sitting in a room for chunks of time, maybe for 12 hours a day, putting together the record and editing it," he said. "I had my friends stop by the studio, and they'd goof around, and we'd [perform] what we wrote or we'd improvise off of that. So I had 15 [to] 20 choices to go over on every skit, and we put together this compilation. That takes a lot of time."

It also took a toll. "And you're always in little rooms, so you go stir crazy . . . you're going, 'What did I do with my life?'" Actually, Adam knew why he spent so much time at work. "You don't want them to take [your success] away from you. So you have to put pressure on your-self to do as good as you can do."

The second album was like Adam's other work: childlike but sometimes rough. "Steve Poly-chronopolous" was a track about a proud bully. On the other hand, "Dip Doodle" was a goofy ode to grandmothers. Predictably, most of the critics disliked the album. Even the loving Judy Sandler was no fan: "My mom, she can't listen to my album. It's too dirty," Adam admitted.

But the album was a hit, selling over two million copies, partly because it contained Adam's most popular tune, "The Chanukah Song." Radio stations had repeatedly played the song during Chanukah the previous year, and that had raised demand for the album.

Along the way, Adam and Margaret Ruden broke up. Neither one discussed the reasons publicly, but Adam has made jokes about him being a jealous boyfriend: "I could have ten girls talking to me, and then one guy comes up to her and says, 'How's it going?' and I'm like, *'What'd that guy say to you? Well, next time don't look at him! You looked at him!'"*

The breakup didn't interrupt Adam's work schedule. The spring of 1996 saw him filming *Bulletproof*, costarring Damon Wayans. The movie mixed action with Adam's usual silliness. Wayans played a cop who had to take a small-time criminal (Adam) from Arizona to Los Angeles. Adam drives the cop nuts by, among other things, singing him a falsetto version of the sappy ballad "I Will Always Love You."

Bulletproof opened in August 1996 to painful reviews. John Anderson of *New York Newsday* called it "your standard vulgar, mindless, action-buddy flick," and *Time*'s Richard Corliss criticized its "plotholes of delirious implausibility."

Nevertheless, *Bulletproof* was the top performer of all movies during its first weekend, earning $6 million. But it couldn't sustain the pace and soon fell out of sight.

When the movie opened, Adam was busy with his summer 1996 tour, and he continued to keep himself busy after the tour as well. *What the Hell Happened to Me?* spawned an HBO comedy special of the same name, airing in October. Around the same time, the album was certified platinum (a million copies sold), and later was certified double platinum. It earned Adam a Grammy nomination for Best Comedy Album of 1996. In the spring of '97,

Adam volunteered to be a prize in a Los Angeles synagogue's charity auction; the winner got to hang out with him.

He was also briefly involved with the development of the movie *Very Bad Things*, but later pulled out of the project because he felt it was too dark for him.

These activities were only side projects. Adam spent most of his time on his next album, which was released in late 1997. *What's Your Name?* was more like Adam's tour than his other two records. It was all songs, with music provided by Waddy Wachtel and Bob Glaub, among other musicians.

Bulletproof, in which Adam costarred with Damon Wayans (right), once again earned brutal reviews. The film was a top box-office hit when it was first released but was soon forgotten.

As always, Adam mixed raw crudeness with a sympathy for the underdog. The album's 14 tracks included "Four Years Old," a slice of life from a young boy's viewpoint; the *Saturday Night Live* favorite "Red Hooded Sweatshirt"; and "Moyda," a tale of a killer. A favorite among fans was "The Lonesome Kicker," which laments the troubles of the football kicker.

The record was another hit—selling half a million copies by the spring of 1999. However, it was nothing compared to Adam's success in the movies. He was earning more than $7 million per film and involved with everything from scripts to casting to editing.

He turned his focus to his next movie, *The Wedding Singer*. "People like to hear Adam sing, and I just got married," said Tim Herlihy, explaining how the movie came to be. Written by Herlihy and Adam with help from Judd Apatow, the romantic comedy featured Adam as a crooner who falls for a sweet waitress.

"Adam deliberately set out to make an Adam Sandler movie that wasn't a typical Adam Sandler movie," said New Line Cinema president Mitch Goldman.

There was a problem, though: Adam wasn't confident enough as a singer to carry the role. He thought people would say, "I just heard that [song] on the radio. Why do I want to hear him singing it?"

Herlihy came up with an idea: instead of using tunes currently on the air, Adam should sing songs that were out of circulation. So they set the film in 1985, when songs like Madonna's self-satisfied "Material Girl" and Billy Idol's snarly "White Wedding" were fresh. "It sort of took the corniness out of me singing," Adam said. "[It] made it a little more nostalgic to hear the tunes. It makes the movie fun." Plus, it opened up new things to make fun of: "We basically partied in the '80s," said producer Robert Simonds.

The movie had to strike a difficult balance, Adam commented. "The ultimate goal was to make people laugh, but my character had to be believably in love." To get his performance right, he studied real-life wedding singers. "It takes a lot of courage to be up there, singing in front of people they don't know," he commented later. To get the proper '80s look, he wore an uncomfortable wig.

It wasn't all work and pain; Adam kept his pals around. With Frank Coraci as director, Jack Giarraputo as producer, and Herlihy and Apatow on the script, everything seemed to go Adam's way.

Then tragedy hit. Adam had never lost touch with his *Saturday Night Live* buddy Chris Farley. The 290-pound comedian, a whirling dervish of noise and laughter who stuffed himself with food, liquor, and drugs, appeared in *Billy Madison* and *Airheads*. He saw Adam's movies on their opening nights, and he always phoned to tell Adam the audiences' reaction and his own opinion. He even dropped in as a guest star on Adam's concert tour.

Adam loved Farley's work. When he saw Farley's movie *Tommy Boy*, "I was laughing my [butt] off watching him." More than that, he loved Farley. "He really, really was automatic happiness whenever I'd see him," Adam said.

And then, shortly before Christmas 1997, Farley was dead from a drug overdose. At age 33, Farley was only a couple of years older than Adam. His death hit Adam hard. "I have never gone through this before," Adam said. "I had

The Wedding Singer *gave Adam the break- through role he'd been searching for. It also contributed to his receiving the ShoWest Comedy Star of the Year Award, which was presented to him by his costar in the film, Drew Barrymore (right).*

grandparents pass away, and that hurts a lot. But that's natural. This is an unnatural death. And I can't stop thinking about it."

He attended Chris Farley's funeral with *SNL* veterans Lorne Michaels and Rob Schneider. "I haven't cried in a long time—I thought I'd forgotten how—but at Farley's funeral, I let it all out because it just hurt so much," Adam expressed. A few days later he visited the *SNL* studio. "My heart hurt. I was thinking of Farley and how much fun we used to have."

While thinking of Farley usually made Adam grieve, it sometimes also cheered him up. "I like thinking of him," Adam said. "I like thinking that he's listening, and I like still trying to make him laugh."

Eventually Adam recovered from his friend's death and returned to work. His efforts paid off in February 1998, when New Line Cinema released *The Wedding Singer*. The critics actually liked it. Michael Rechtshaffen of the *Hollywood Reporter* called the movie "a (for the most part) winning romantic comedy." Showbiz journalist Jeanne Wolf described Adam's work in the film as "an endearing, show-stealing performance." "It's a perfect part for him," wrote the *Chicago Tribune*'s Richard Christiansen.

By earning almost $22 million in its first weekend, *The Wedding Singer* became America's second most popular movie of that weekend, right behind the blockbuster *Titanic*. And it stayed strong, taking in more than $80 million overall.

Still, Adam remained insecure. "I have my doubts all the time. I'll be happy, and then I'll get panicky and say, 'Why am I doing this?'" Even with his comedy, he admitted, "I don't know what the hell I'm doing." However, he felt secure enough to accept big money. Around the time *The Wedding Singer* was opening in theaters, Adam signed another movie deal for $12.5 million, agreeing to make the film that would later be titled *Big Daddy*.

But before that film could be shot, there was yet another one to make.

7

BOBBY, SONNY,
AND THE FUTURE

"**H**e's a guy who got picked on his whole life, and never fought back," Adam said of Bobby, the character he played in *The Waterboy*. "And finally Henry Winkler, as the coach, says, 'You're allowed to fight back, son.' He fights back, it turns out he has a lot of pent-up anger, and he tackles this guy pretty hard. So the coach puts him on the team as a linebacker."

After the long, hard stress of making *The Wedding Singer*, *The Waterboy* was a return to form: a slapstick comedy about a put-upon loser. There was even a hint of Cajunman in that Bobby came from the Louisiana bayou, Cajunman's home.

Also familiar to Adam were the people behind the scenes. Adam wrote the movie with Tim Herlihy. Frank Coraci directed, and Jack Giarraputo and Robert Simonds were along as producers. Other friends filled other roles, on-screen and off.

Their presence may have helped Adam. Despite Adam's comments about being insecure, Winkler found him confident. "I watched him as he heard the material being read,

The Waterboy, *in which Adam starred with Henry Winkler (left), was a huge box-office hit and raised Adam's salary to $20 million a movie. This fee puts him in elite company with Tom Cruise and Mel Gibson.*

and Adam was in complete charge of every joke. He knew if it worked or if it didn't."

Yet he was no dictator. "The set was very jokey, very up and funny and light," said Fairuza Balk, who played Bobby's girlfriend. Adam commented, "I had the best time making this—I got to hang out with my buddies, throw a football around, and I had a lot of fun tackling people. It was fun pretending I'm tough."

The Waterboy got the usual criticisms. Some were mild: "The patented Sandler formula still works, darn it," wrote the *Hollywood Reporter's* Michael Rechtshaffen. Others were harsher. The *New York Post* wrote: "Adam Sandler's latest comedy is pure pain." Even fellow *Saturday Night Live* veteran Bill Murray threw in a harsh criticism: "I would enjoy driving in L.A. [smog] with the windows open more than I would enjoy watching *The Waterboy.*"

The movie came out in November, in time for the lucrative holiday movie-going season. It earned nearly $160 million before it left theaters for home video. Adam's fee rose to $20 million per movie, putting him in the same rank as Tom Cruise and Mel Gibson.

Even with all his successes, Adam continued to say that he couldn't relax. "When you're a comedian, the problem is that there is no middle," he said. "You're either pretty damned excited about something or pretty damned depressed about something else. Honestly, every part of my life is tough. I make it tough on myself. I get nervous. I want to do as good as I can do."

Adam remained a lightning rod for controversy. During a seminar on comedy at the screenwriters' union, the Writers Guild of America, Adam became a topic of attack. "It's like Bob Hope," said Albert Brooks, a respected writer, director, and former stand-up. "I don't remember ever laughing at him."

Adam probably didn't care. About that time he started dating actress-model Jacqueline Titone, whom he quickly fell for. "I really do want to grow old with [her]," he said, and at the same time he was busy with his next movie, *Big Daddy*.

Initially, Adam didn't want to do the movie, which originated as a screenplay called *Guy Gets Kid* by writer Steve Franks. According to Amy Pascal, president of Columbia Pictures, the story about a bachelor who adopts a five-year-old boy had been sitting around Columbia for years.

Pascal decided that Adam was right for the movie when she saw an early version of *The Wedding Singer*. "I followed him around and stalked him," Pascal joked. She tracked him to Atlantic City, where Adam was playing slot machines with his dad. Pascal approached Adam, and he said no, but Pascal didn't quit. She set up another meeting with him. "Adam said, 'I'm not gonna do it,' and as he was walking out the door—and I was really devastated—he said, 'You know how we could make it work? We could make it work if we changed it so that I adopt the kid to get my girlfriend back.'"

With that idea in mind, Adam and Tim Herlihy rewrote the script. Adam's character, Sonny Koufax, would rather live like a dorm slob than make something of his life, much to his girlfriend's annoyance. He adopts a five-year-old boy; although that move doesn't make the girlfriend love him, it does force Sonny to grow up and attracts an even better woman.

Big Daddy was shot in New York during the

fall and winter of 1998. The cast included friends from Adam's stand-up days, including Jon Stewart and Rob Schneider. "Adam called me up and said, 'Hey, there's a role in this movie for ya, Delivery Guy,'" Schneider recalled. "I go, 'What role? There's no role! It's two lines and the guy's Chinese right now!' He said, 'Doesn't matter. Come out, it'll be fun.'" Eventually Schneider's role became one of the funniest in the movie.

The mood on the set was light. During wardrobe fittings, Adam broke into silly songs. Instead of the traditional star trailer (essentially a motor home) Adam used an oversized tour bus and held rock 'n' roll jam sessions in it. He gave Dylan and Cole Sprouse, the twins who played Sonny's son, a pinball machine. "They like Adam," said Schneider. "He'd yell at them, and they'd just laugh." Joey Lauren Adams, who played Adam's love interest, said, "He's like a big kid—a kid who never grew up."

The big kid was also the boss. "It was Adam who was the arbiter of what was funny and what wasn't," costume designer Ellen Lutter said. The director, Dennis Dugan, agreed: "Adam works with the editing, the writing—everything." When Adam wanted a song from the band Limp Bizkit for the movie, he didn't have an assistant or executive contact the band; he talked directly with Limp Bizkit lead singer Fred Durst.

When *Big Daddy* opened in June 1999, the critics made their usual attacks. Even the ads provoked anger, as they featured Sonny teaching his son to use a wall as a public restroom and infuriated the more proper people who saw them.

As usual, what the critics said didn't matter

to Adam or his fans. Within three months, *Big Daddy* took in $160 million.

As *Big Daddy* was filling theaters, Adam was back where he hadn't been in more than a year: the recording studio. Like his first two records, *Stan and Judy's Kid* was a collection of sketches and songs. It featured the "Chanukah Song, Part 2," a sequel to his most famous tune. It even included a song backed by Frank Sinatra's band.

The record helped Adam into a new world: animation. Adam and his friend Allen Covert (a stand-up comic who has acted in Adam's movies) wrote, produced, and released on the Internet a six-minute cartoon based on the track "The Peeper."

The cartoon gave Adam animation experience that he would soon need. Earlier in the year, he had signed a deal with Sony Pictures

The 1999 movie Big Daddy *reunited Adam with his friend Rob Schneider (left). Critics panned the film, but Adam ignored their comments, focusing instead on the $160 million the movie brought in during its first three months of release.*

Adam Sandler's popularity brings many invitations to make public appearances. Here, (from left to right) ESPN Sports Center anchor Kenny Mayne, Adam, actress Kathy Bates, figure skater Michelle Kwan, and Walt Disney Company Chairman and CEO Michael Eisner come together to celebrate the opening of Disney's ESPN Zone in Baltimore.

to produce (with Jack Giarraputo) a cartoon movie musical starring an animated version of himself.

Up next for Adam is a film called *Little Nicky*, a story of a young man (Adam) forced to go into his father's business. His father is Satan. Mike De Luca, a top executive at New Line Cinema, describes *Little Nicky* as "a special-effects comedy like *Ghostbusters*."

Meanwhile, Adam formed a production company of his own, Happy Madison, and branched out into making movies that he doesn't star in. He was one of the producers of the recent movie about an inept gigolo, *Deuce Bigalow: Male*

Gigolo, written by and starring Rob Schneider.

For all his success, Adam remains a grown-up boy. Even though he has expensive homes in Los Angeles and New York, they're filled with toys and games. His tastes aren't fancy: "As long as he has a blanket and a tiny, little mattress, he's happy," Frank Coraci has said. "He's the most basic guy." His wardrobe is T-shirts, jeans, sweats, and sneakers. "Everybody wants me to dress up, and I can't do it," he has said.

What about the future? While Adam was making *Big Daddy*, there was a rumor that he would marry Jackie Titone. (He didn't.) When *Big Daddy* opened, Adam was asked about fatherhood. "I'll try my best, but I'll still be lousy," he responded.

Adam has described his early years as "doing something wrong, getting yelled at and making the person laugh. Then it would be all right."

That sounds like a nearly perfect life for a comedian who's both a supremely strong comedic mind and a mischievous little boy all at the same time.

CHRONOLOGY

1966 Born in Brooklyn, New York, to Stan and Judy Sandler on September 9.

1972 Family moves to Manchester, New Hampshire.

1984 Begins performing stand-up comedy at Stitches in Boston; attends New York University in New York City; meets Tim Herlihy, who will become his best friend and cowriter.

1985 Plays the Comic Strip and other comedy clubs in the New York area.

1987 Gets a recurring role on *The Cosby Show*.

1988 Joins the cast of the MTV game show *Remote Control*.

1989 Meets Margaret Ruden; moves to Los Angeles and performs at the city's comedy clubs; makes his first movie, *Babes Ahoy* (also known as *Going Overboard*).

1990 Joins the writing staff at *Saturday Night Live (SNL)*, and occasionally performs on the show.

1991 Becomes a full-fledged cast member of *SNL*; does stand-up shows during breaks from *SNL*; plays a small part in movie *Shakes the Clown*.

1993 Records his first album, *they're all gonna laugh at you!*; takes a small part in the *SNL* movie *Coneheads*.

1994 Films *Airheads* and *Mixed Nuts*; cowrites and films *Billy Madison*.

1995 Receives Grammy nomination for Best Comedy Album for *they're all gonna laugh at you!*; proposes marriage to Margaret Ruden; quits *SNL*; cowrites and films *Happy Gilmore*; records his second album, *What the Hell Happened to Me?*; performs stand-up at various colleges.

1996 Ends his engagement with Margaret Ruden; costars in *Bulletproof*; goes on the road with a comedy-and-music concert tour; records his third album, *What's Your Name?*; receives Grammy nomination for Best Comedy Album for *What the Hell Happened to Me?*

1997 *What's Your Name?* is released; friend Chris Farley dies; *The Wedding Singer* is filmed.

1998 Cowrites and stars in *The Waterboy*; dates actress/model Jackie Titone; cowrites and films *Big Daddy*.

1999   Records *Stan and Judy's Kid*; releases an animated-cartoon
         version of the *Stan and Judy's Kid* track "The Peeper"; signs a deal
         to make a feature-length animated cartoon; works on the movie
         Little Nicky; sets up his own production company, Happy Madison,
         which produces the movie *Deuce Bigalow: Male Gigolo*; accepts
         Comedy Star of the Year Award at ShoWest; receives MTV Award
         for Best Comedic Performance for his role in *The Waterboy*.

ACCOMPLISHMENTS

Film

1989   *Babes Ahoy* (also known as *Going Overboard*)

1991   *Shakes the Clown*

1993   *Coneheads*

1994   *Airheads*
         Mixed Nuts

1995   *Billy Madison*

1996   *Happy Gilmore*
         Bulletproof

1998   *The Wedding Singer*
         The Waterboy

1999   *Big Daddy*

Television

1987   *The Cosby Show* (guest star)

1988–89 *Remote Control*

1990–95 *Saturday Night Live*

Albums

1993   *they're all gonna laugh at you!*

1996   *What the Hell Happened to Me?*

1997   *What's Your Name?*
1999   *Stan and Judy's Kid*

Further Reading

Berkman, Meredith. "Adam Sandler is a Very Funny Guy." *Mademoiselle*, March 1995.

Cader, Michael (editor). *Saturday Night Live: The First Twenty Years*. Boston: Houghton Mifflin, 1994.

Meyers, Kate. "Adam Ribs." *Entertainment Weekly*, February 17, 1995.

Salem, Jon. *Adam Sandler: Not Too Shabby!* New York: Scholastic Inc., 1999.

Schneider, Karen. "Last Laugh." *People*, November 30, 1998.

Stiller, Ben. "Adam Sandler." *Interview*, December 1994.

Willman, Chris. "Just Call Him Bankable Boy." *Los Angeles Times*, July 10, 1994.

About the Author

DAVID SEIDMAN is a journalist who has written about entertainment for the *Los Angeles Times*, *San Francisco Examiner*, and other publications. His books include *All Gone: Things That Aren't There Anymore* and the upcoming *Young Zillionaire's Guide to Supply and Demand*. He lives in Los Angeles.

Acknowledgment

This book would not be possible without the work of dozens of journalists who covered Adam Sandler before I came along. Adam no longer talks to print journalists, including unauthorized biographers, and he's asked his friends and family to do the same. So much of the information in this book comes from my colleagues. Thanks to one and all.

INDEX

PHOTO CREDITS:

Brenda Chase/OLUSA: 2, 10; Kevin Mazur/London Features Int'l: 6; Warner Bros./NMI: 8; New Millennium Images: 13, 18, 26, 34; Jim Sulley/PR NewsFoto: 22; Allen Gordon/London Features Int'l: 25; Justin Sutcliffe/AP/Wide World Photos: 28; Everett Collection: 31, 37, 42, 47, 52; Universal Studio/NMI: 40; Ethan Miller/Reuters: 50; Columbia/TriStar/NMI: 57; FPS/PR NewsFoto: 58.